Milly, Mr Mills and the Marvellous Music

Written by Wendy Meddour
Illustrated by Tatsiana Burgaud

OXFORD
UNIVERSITY PRESS

Words to look out for ...

combine *(verb)*
combines, combining, combined

To combine things is to join them or mix them together.

contradict *(verb)*
contradicts, contradicting, contradicted

To contradict someone (or something) is to say they are wrong or untrue.

due *(adjective)*
expected to arrive at a particular time

eliminate *(verb)*
eliminates, eliminating, eliminated

To eliminate someone (or something) is to get rid of them.

obvious *(adjective)*
easy to see or understand

relate *(verb)*
relates, relating, related

Things relate when they are connected or linked in some way.

Chapter 1

Milly lived in a flat, right above her mum's fancy-dress shop. Mr Minto lived in the flat opposite Milly, right above his shoe shop.

Sometimes, Milly waved at Mr Minto from her balcony. Mr Minto always waved back.

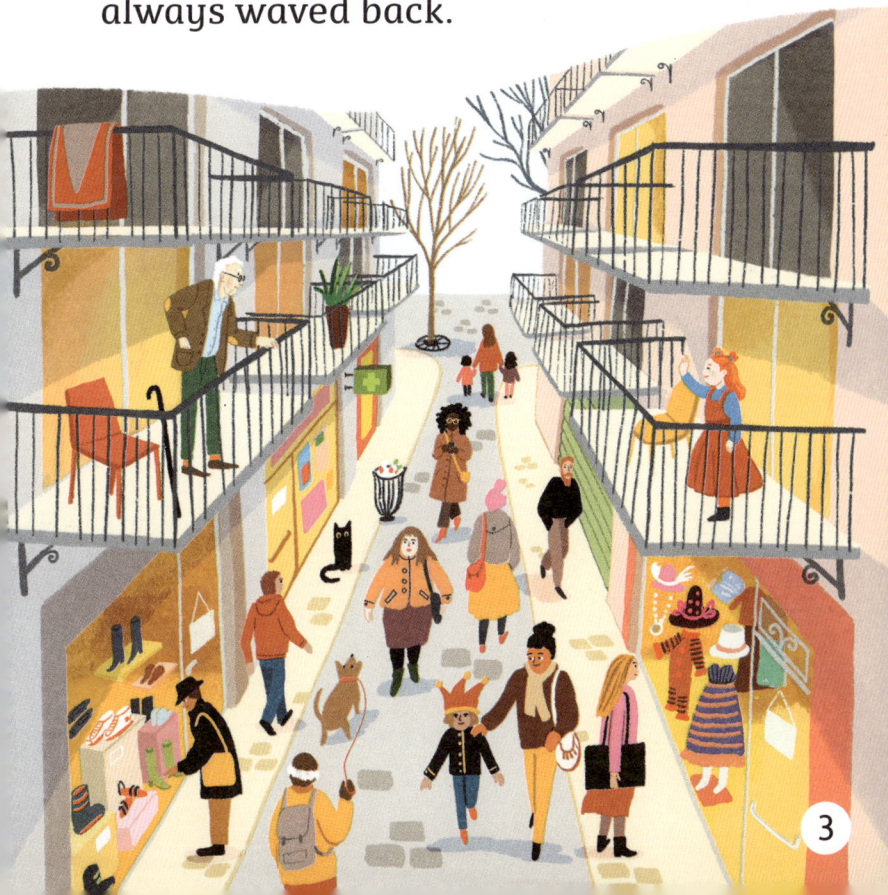

One rainy Saturday, Milly's mum, Sarah, was working in her shop. There wasn't much for Milly to do. Milly sat down and sighed.

'Come and help me with these boxes,' Mum said. The boxes were full of colourful clothes and hats.

Milly picked up a large box.
'What's inside this one?' she asked.

'Why don't you open it?' suggested Mum.

Milly opened the box. Inside, there was a black case. Milly carefully lifted it out.

'Can you guess what's inside the case?' asked Mum.

Milly thought about it then tried to eliminate a few things. 'It's too heavy to be a box of clothes,' she said.

To eliminate someone (or something) is to get rid of them.

'I'll give you a clue,' said Mum. 'Toot!'

'That's not a very obvious clue,' giggled Milly. 'Is it a toy car?'

Mum shook her head and laughed. 'No. Why don't you have a look?' she said.

Milly opened the case and saw that it was …

'A trumpet!' Milly exclaimed.

When something is obvious, it is easy to see or understand.

Milly had wanted a trumpet ever since she'd seen someone playing one in the town square.

'It's not perfect,' said Milly's mum. 'It's old, but it's been cleaned.'

Milly contradicted her. 'It IS perfect!' she said, hugging her mum. 'Can we go up to the flat and try it out?'

'Of course!' Mum said.

To contradict someone (or something) is to say they are wrong or untrue.

Chapter 2

The flat was small so Milly took her trumpet out onto the balcony. She put the metal to her lips and blew hard.

'What's that noise? I'm trying to work!' shouted Mrs Stern, from a balcony above.

'Sorry, Mrs Stern,' Milly said. 'I am learning to play.'

'Maybe try another day, Milly,' suggested Mum.

So that is what Milly did. She practised *every* morning before school and *every* night after school.

'Please stop!' called Mr Tanaka, who lived above Milly. 'I'm trying to paint!'

'The twins were trying to sleep!' said Ms Grant, who lived next door.

Milly didn't hear them. Her trumpet was too loud.

By the weekend, Milly's neighbours were fed up. They gathered for a meeting in Mr Minto's shoe shop.

'I haven't done a painting all week,' said Mr Tanaka.

'The twins have hardly slept,' grumbled Ms Grant.

'I know how they feel,' replied Mr Minto, taking cotton wool out of his ears.

'Is there anything we can do to eliminate the noise?' Mrs Stern asked.

Milly's neighbours couldn't think of a solution.

'Leave it to me,' said Mr Minto, smiling.

To eliminate someone (or something) is to get rid of them.

11

Chapter 3

The next day, Mr Minto searched under his bed.

'Ah! There you are,' he said, pulling out a black case.

Then he went out onto his balcony.

'Milly!' he shouted.

Milly stopped playing and put her trumpet down.

'Hello, Mr Minto! I think my trumpet's broken,' she said.

'I don't think it's broken,' said Mr Minto. 'Is anybody helping you to learn how to play?'

'No,' said Milly. 'I'm learning all by myself.'

'I see,' said Mr Minto. 'Well, I think I can help you.'

Mr Minto opened his black case. Inside was an ENORMOUS instrument.

'Wow,' gasped Milly. 'That's a big trumpet!'

Mr Minto smiled. 'This is a trombone. Trombones and trumpets are brass instruments,' he said. 'I blow into it and make a buzzing sound with my lips.'

Mr Minto took a deep breath and began to blow. He made a wonderful sound!

'It's beautiful!' Milly exclaimed. 'Will you show me how to play like that?'

'Of course … if it's OK with your mum,' said Mr Minto.

That evening, Mr Minto went to Milly's flat. Milly's mum was delighted with Mr Minto's plan.

Chapter 4

The next day, Milly raced home from school. She waited on the balcony. Mr Minto was due to arrive for their lesson at any moment.

First, Mr Minto taught Milly how to hold the trumpet properly. Then he showed her how to press her lips together to make a clear sound.

If you are due to arrive at a particular time, you are expected to arrive at that time.

It wasn't easy at first. Milly's mouth ached.

'Don't give up, Milly. Remember, the sound that comes out of the trumpet relates to the way your lips are shaped,' Mr Minto said.

The neighbours still complained.

'Mr Minto, I thought you were going to help!' said Ms Grant.

'Can we please have some peace around here?' asked Mr Tanaka.

Things relate when they are connected or linked in some way.

However, it wasn't long before things started to change. Milly got better at playing the trumpet! Mr Minto sometimes played his trombone at the same time.

'How magnificent!' cried Mr Tanaka. 'When you combine the sounds of the instruments, it makes me want to paint!'

18 To combine things is to join them or mix them together.

Later that week, Mr Minto noticed Mrs Stern was peering over her balcony.

'That sounds beautiful,' Mrs Stern said. 'Your music made me want to get out my old bugle. I've not played it for years, but can I join in?'

'Of course you can,' Milly said, with a smile.

The next day, Ms Grant appeared on her balcony. 'This looks fun! Can the twins join in?' she asked.

'Why not?' Mr Minto replied, looking across at Ms Grant. 'Have you got any instruments?'

'They could use these saucepan lids,' said Ms Grant.

'Perfect!' Mr Minto replied, laughing.

'I don't have a trumpet,' said Ms Grant. 'But I can play the spoons!'

'Great,' Milly replied, giggling. 'You can all join in!'

By the following week, lots of Milly's neighbours had found something to make music with. Some instruments had been forgotten about for years!

Milly counted all the instruments. There were three tubas, three trombones, four trumpets, one bugle, four saucepan lids and fourteen spoons!

'This is the most fun I've had in ages,' said Mr Tanaka.

'Me too,' tooted Mrs Stern.

'Let's play our instruments together every Wednesday night,' suggested Mr Minto.

Chapter 5

Word soon travelled around the town. Every Wednesday evening, a crowd of people began to gather on the street to listen.

Everyone agreed that Milly and Mr Minto's music was wonderful. The crowd cheered and clapped. 'More! More!' they shouted.

There was just one obvious problem.

When something is obvious, it is easy to see or understand.

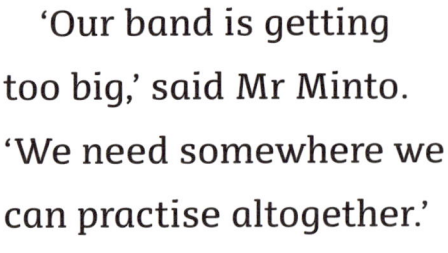

'Our band is getting too big,' said Mr Minto. 'We need somewhere we can practise altogether.'

'What shall we do?' asked Milly.

'I wonder if we could use the bandstand in the park. I used to love playing there as a boy,' Mr Minto said.

'I remember that old bandstand,' said Mum. 'I think it needs fixing up. The wood is old and the paint is peeling.'

Milly looked thoughtful. Then she picked a ball of string off the table.

'Have we got any spare hats and some needles?' Milly asked. 'I think I have a plan!'

That evening, Milly, Mr Minto and Mum got to work. They sewed string onto each hat. Then they delivered one to each band member.

The following week, people gathered again to listen. After their practice ended, Milly asked the band members to lower their hats. People began to throw coins into the hats. Milly's heart filled with joy.

It didn't take long before the band had enough money to buy ...

... a box of nails,

two hammers,

and some paint and paintbrushes.

They even had enough money left to buy some shakers, triangles and drums.

Milly and her mum put a sign on the window of the fancy-dress shop.

Dear friends,

Please come and help us fix the bandstand! Meet at 10 o'clock this Saturday in the park.

Love Milly and Mr Minto

Chapter 6

On Saturday, lots of people turned up to help.

Ms Grant mended the floor.

Mr Tanaka painted the metal columns.

Mrs Stern made a new sign.

With a huge team effort, they fixed up the old bandstand.

Mr Minto beamed at Milly. 'It looks as good as new!' he said.

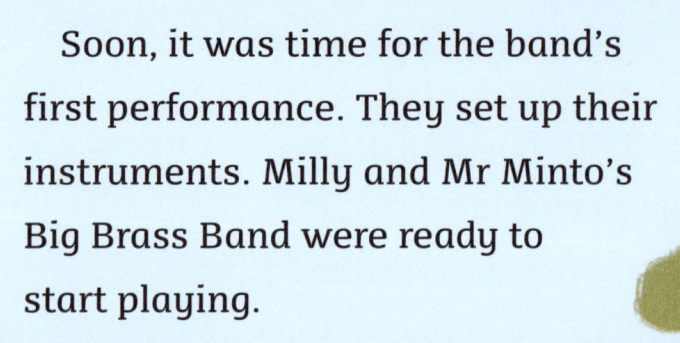

Soon, it was time for the band's first performance. They set up their instruments. Milly and Mr Minto's Big Brass Band were ready to start playing.

Everyone in the band thought Milly and Mr Minto were marvellous.

Come and join our band every Saturday. Please help yourself to an instrument!

The combined sound of the instruments had never been so beautiful. Music filled the air.

Tum tee tum tee tum ...

'More, more, more!' shouted the crowd.

'You're the best trumpet player that I know, Milly,' beamed Mr Minto.

To combine things is to join them or mix them together.

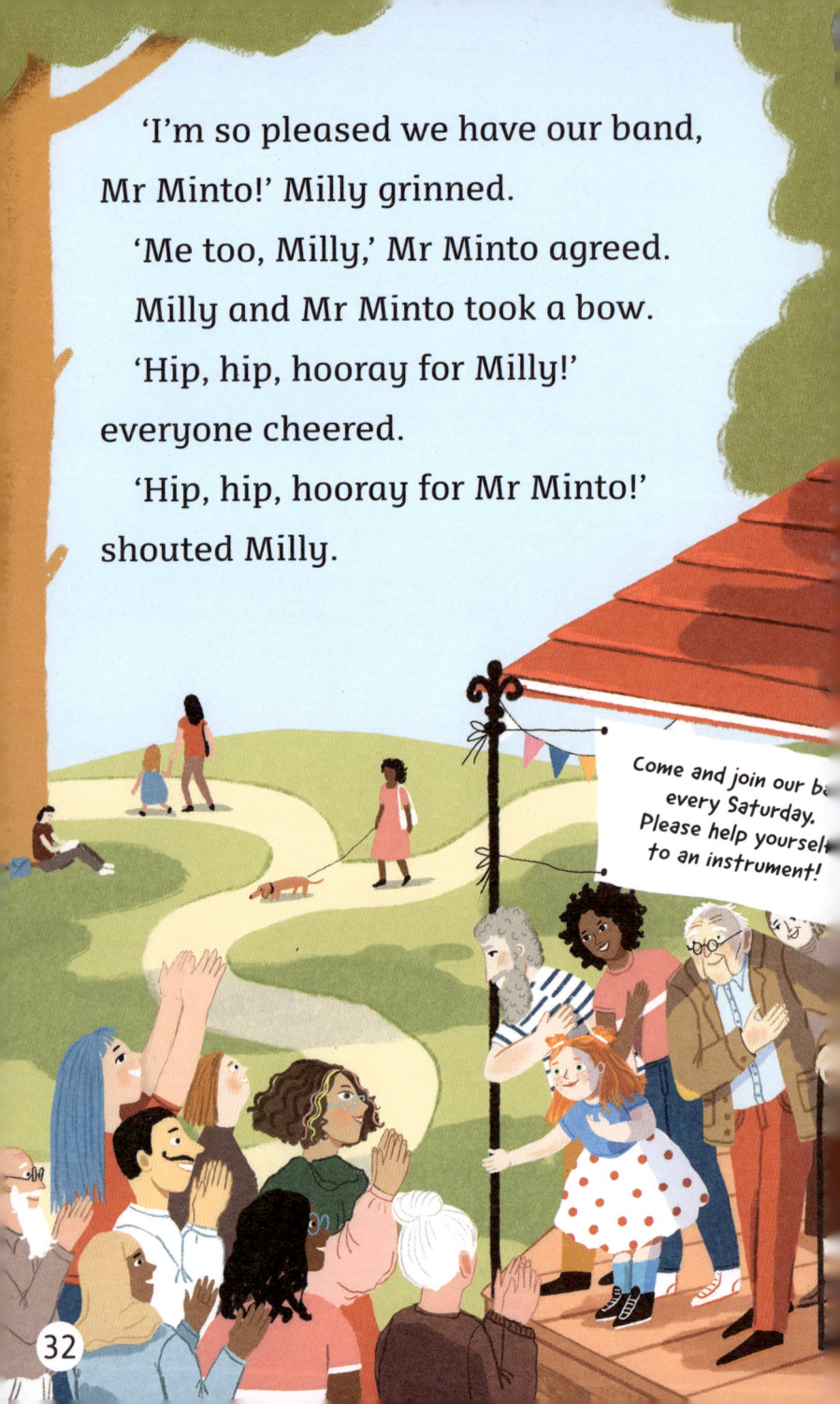

'I'm so pleased we have our band, Mr Minto!' Milly grinned.

'Me too, Milly,' Mr Minto agreed.

Milly and Mr Minto took a bow.

'Hip, hip, hooray for Milly!' everyone cheered.

'Hip, hip, hooray for Mr Minto!' shouted Milly.

Come and join our b[and]
every Saturday.
Please help yoursel[f]
to an instrument!